T

NEAT A

GUI

LEWES

The hanging sign outside Andy & Marvin's barber shop in Fisher Street was fashioned in the forge next door.

David Arscott

First published in 2005 by S.B. Publications,
14 Bishopstone Road, Seaford, East Sussex BN25 2UB

ISBN 1-85770-308-1

Printed by Ethos Productions Ltd.

Front Cover: View of Lewes from Golf Course (courtesy of
Chloe Gillett)

INTRODUCTION

This book follows the established format of what has become a popular series, taking the reader through the streets of Lewes in a more or less logical direction and highlighting striking and curious features along the way. I am, of course, well aware that the required brevity may be regarded as a vice as well as a virtue, but there are other volumes (*see page 66*) which deal with the fascinating history of our East Sussex county town in meaty detail. This little guide is a taster for those in a hurry.

We begin in Cliffe, an area which once lay outside the town's boundaries and, indeed, in a different Norman administrative division, or rape. We then steadily climb the east-west ridge of the downland spur on which Lewes rests, with occasional excursions to either side. Please note that the sketch map of the town on page 72 and the smaller ones within the text are not drawn to scale.

Lewes is a town which punches above its weight. Its population is only around 15,000, but it has crown courts, the county hall, a Norman castle, a river with working wharves, a brewery and a prison. Its long high street, largely unspoilt, is lined with houses of a great age and displaying a wide variety of building materials.

Repeatedly touched by national events, Lewes has sometimes helped shape them too, with a special reputation for being in the forefront of dissent, both religious and political – the brave defiance of the Protestant martyrs, the rallying to Parliament by local gentry in the Civil War, the revolutionary tracts of Thomas Paine. At Lewes, moreover, Simon de Montfort defeated a king and put a match to the slow-burning fuse of democracy.

This rich story has been told in detail and at length elsewhere. Here's an invitation to enjoy a brief glimpse of it on foot.

DAVID ARSCOTT
LEWES, 2005

The river approach to Lewes from the south, with South Street on the right. The Ouse was once important to the town commercially, and there are still wharves on its banks today.

SOUTH STREET

We begin our trail along a street which was, until the opening of the Cuilfail tunnel in December 1980, the main thoroughfare into the town from the south. Today it's a cul-de-sac with its own riverside flavour – some of the house names evoke the days when boats came up from the sea to unload here and when there were pubs called the Bargeman's Arms and The Schooner.

The Snowdrop Inn, at the end of the street, is named (with a somewhat macabre touch) for the catastrophic avalanche of December 27, 1836, which engulfed the terraced cottages of Boulder Row – the local poor house – and claimed eight lives. Craning our necks to the downland cliff that rears overhead, it's all too easy to imagine the impact of that smothering bank of snow. At the time, however, the inhabitants felt secure

The Snowdrop Inn, the site of Britain's most deadly avalanche.

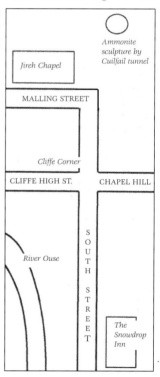

in their homes and ignored urgent warnings that they should leave. The dead (ranging in age from 15 to 82) were buried at South Malling church, where a plaque refers to 'an awful instance of the uncertainty of human life'. Relics of the tragedy, including the dress of a little girl whose life was saved, can be seen in the Anne of Cleves House museum in Southover.

Ship's prow behind the bar of the Snowdrop Inn.

CHAPEL HILL

Once called East Street, Chapel Hill entices the passer-by with its collection of attractive slate- and tile-hung houses disappearing around a bend on a slope which becomes much steeper further

up. An ancient downland route to Glynde and Ringmer, it takes you up to the golf course and, via a footpath off to your left, to the obelisk which remembers the seventeen Protestant martyrs whose story we shall tell later on.

The current street name derives from a former chapel built here by Calvanistic Methodists around 1775. A number of disaffected members broke away to found the Jireh Chapel.

MALLING STREET

Here's a street which has been cruelly cut in two by major road changes. At the Dorset Arms, named for the Sackville family, Earls of Dorset, who had long connections with the town, the road now veers sharply left to pass by the side of the Jireh Chapel. Originally it ran straight on, past the front of the chapel (the attractive gateway, made at the Lewes Foundry, has been

moved) and what is now the opening of the Cuilfail tunnel and – the numbering resumes here – up the hill towards Ringmer.

The chapel dates from 1805, built by the Rev J. Jenkins W.A (he was a self-styled 'Welsh Ambassador of God's Truth') with, as a plaque tells us, 'the voluntary contributions of the CITIZENS of ZION'. Another evangelist is buried here: William Huntington S.S. ('Sinner Saved')

Above: The Dorset Arms (popularly known as The Cats) displays the Sackville family's heraldic leopards on its sign.

Right: The Jireh Chapel with its ornate gateway.

Below: The resting place of the coal heaver who rejoiced in being a 'sinner saved'.

devised his own epitaph which can still be read today. He was 'beloved of his God but abhorred of men'. Fortunately, however, 'the Omniscient Judge at the Grand Assize shall ratify and confirm this to the confusion of many thousands, for England and its metropolis shall know that there hath been a prophet among them.'

The chapel itself, expensively restored, is a large, barn-like building with mathematical tiles on a base of chequered bricks. The strain of vigorous evangelicanism practised at the Jireh makes it no surprise that this remains a centre of nonconformist dissent, and that a thanksgiving service is held here each November 5 as a prelude to the town's famously anarchic bonfire celebrations. A delicate balance is held between pope-burning and giving no offence to today's Roman Catholics, and there was a great fuss a few years ago when the peppery Rev Ian Paisley was invited.

The ammonite sculpture on the roundabout outside the Cuilfail tunnel.

Skirt the building and you'll have a view of the Cuilfail tunnel and the continuation of Malling Street: an ammonite sculpture grudgingly accepted by locals sits on the traffic island nearby. The tunnel gets its name from the modern estate of houses on the hill above (reached from a ramp close to the Dorset Arms). Its developer, Isaac Vinall, for some reason gave it the name of a holiday village south of Oban.

CLIFFE HIGH STREET

If you were born and bred there you'll no doubt think yourself a Cliffite first and a Lewesian second. In the early days of the downland settlement Cliffe was a separate community over the river, and the Normans, who divided the county into administrative divisions called rapes, allotted it to the lord of Pevensey rather than William de Warenne, who held Lewes. In 1409 Henry IV granted a charter to 'the town of Cliffe', allowing it

The old parish pump.

to hold a market every Wednesday and fairs twice a year – a facsimile hangs in the porch of St Thomas a Becket church.

    The church is thought to have been founded by the canons of South Malling late in the twelfth century. The scant remains of their monastery lie (in private hands) on the east bank of the Ouse. It was there, according to legend, that the four knights who

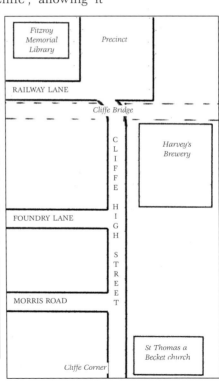

Henry IV's charter.

St Thomas a Becket church.

had murdered Archbishop Becket arrived for the night on their flight to France: when they put their swords on a table (now in the Anne of Cleves House kitchen) it began to shake in protest, throwing their weapons to the floor.

Outside the church you can see the former parish pump and, on the 15th century tower, a clock made by a Ditchling blacksmith in 1670.

There are several venerable buildings on this side of the street, but the frontages on the other side were set back in 1829 in response to a growing volume of traffic: some things never change.

Harvey's is a great survivor – the only Sussex brewery to have greeted the 21st century, and in very good heart at that, with dozens of tied pubs and a capacity of 50,000 barrels a year. Although it's been on its riverside site since the Georgian era most of the present building dates from 1880. Workmen preparing the site for redevelopment discovered the graceful weather vane of 1621 which sits atop the building: it presumably came from a local church.

The company has certainly known its tribulations. In 1875, for instance, a typhoid epidemic swept through Lewes, claiming 30 lives, and the head brewer noted in his journal that the river water used for the brewing process was covered with 'a filthy scum'. No matter: 'We used it in brewing, purifying it by boiling, fermenting, etc., turning out a pure beer.'

The present head brewer, Miles Jenner, has proved himself adept at turning disaster into opportunity. When part of the building was badly damaged by fire in 1997 he brought out a special amber-coloured brew called Firecracker, using highly roasted malts to give 'a slightly burnt quality and a hint of smoke'. After the floods of 2000 swept through the brewery and inundated many homes in the Cliffe and Malling areas, he responded by creating a one-off Ouse Booze.

The floods of 1960 and 2000 were the worst in living memory, but they certainly weren't the first. The original timber bridge over the Ouse was swept away by flood waters in 1727, to be replaced by today's elegant arched structure of brick and stone.

It was on the medieval bridge that St Richard of Chichester is credited with working one of his numerous miracles, blessing the nets of local fishermen so that they caught four mullet – sea-fish which wouldn't normally have been found upstream.

Harvey's Brewery offers fascinating guided tours, which of course include a sampling.

Cliffe Bridge from the south. Pleasure boats predominate today.

As you cross the bridge, take a glance to either side and try to imagine the river crammed with barges, its banks busy with trade, commerce and manufacture – ironworks, warehouses, shipyards and factories. That's how it was in Victorian times, but things are much quieter now. Upstream you'll see Harvey's brewery wharf on the right and Parsons timber yard on the left: Eastgate stone yard and the Phoenix Iron Works once lay beyond it. Downstream on the right, beyond Town Wharf, there's a small reminder of former activity in three warehouses. One of them, Stricklands, was in a sad condition until recent times, when it was restored and, perhaps inevitably, converted to housing.

From Stricklands you can take an attractive detour through the Railway Land nature reserve off to the right. Here, on what was for many years an unconsidered tract of wasteland where the trains had long since ceased to run, a conservation trust set out to establish a haven for wildlife – and with great success. This is a good place to see kingfishers and a range of butterflies. The trust's latest initiative has been a joint arts/wildlife project to create a reedbed which will increase the variety of bird and insect life on the reserve.

Stricklands warehouse – a former granary now given over to housing.

Back at the bridge, we are officially in the High Street once we cross to the west (the houses are numbered accordingly), but the creation of what has become a busy pedestrian precinct here in 1990 disguises the fact. It was, alas, a missed opportunity. 'With the splendid exceptions of Dial House and Fitzroy,' the Friends of Lewes commented at the time, 'this is the one stretch of the High Street with no architectural interest or merit.'

The Congregational Tabernacle, demolished in 1954, stood on the site now occupied by Superdrug.

Dial House, built around 1740, was at one time the home of the Quaker corn merchant Thomas Rickman, and it's thought that he was probably responsible for dividing it in two around 1807. As for the Caen stone facing, that may have been taken from the former friary opposite.

Dial House (nos 220–221 High Street) has a sundial on its pediment with the motto Nosce Te Ipsum – Know Thyself.

The site at Eastgate corner has seen multiple uses. Five hundred years ago there was a Franciscan friary between the east gate and the river. That was closed down as part of Henry VIII's Dissolution of the Monasteries throughout the realm. In 1673 Thomas Pellatt, a merchant, built himself a town house in the picturesque remains. Later, when Sir Fernando Poole owned it, the Prince Regent was a frequent visitor, and William IV and Queen Adelaide came here on an official visit in 1830.

The house was demolished when the town's first railway station was built close by, and in 1862 the Fizroy Memorial Library rose here – designed in the Venetian Gothic style by Sir George Gilbert Scott and financed by one of Baron Nathan Rothschild's daughters, Hannah, in memory of her late husband, the MP for Lewes, Henry Fitzroy.

FITZROY HOUSE
FORMER MEMORIAL LIBRARY
TO HON. HENRY FITZROY M.P.
FOR LEWES 1837-1860. BUILT
1862 BY HIS WIDOW
(ARCHITECT SIR
GEORGE GILBERT
SCOTT.) IT STANDS
ON PART OF THE
SITE OF THE
GREY FRIARS
(DISSOLVED 1538)   19 83

EASTGATE STREET

You don't feel close to the river when visiting the Waitrose supermarket, but the original buildings along Eastgate Street had yards running down to the Ouse. The chestnut tree outside the store is a remarkable survivor of the planners' brutal remaking of this part of town, and Eastgate House close by was saved only after ardent lobbying by conservationists. Built in 1823, it housed the offices of the Eastgate Stoneworks, founded by Arthur Morris around 1750 – an Art Nouveau inscription (suitably carved in stone) declares it to have been 'established over a century'. Memorials created here can be seen in churchyards all over East Sussex.

The chestnut outside the supermarket is a brave survivor of drastic changes in the area.

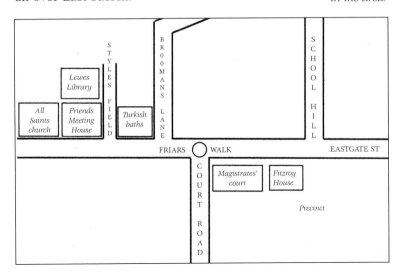

The former Eastgate Stoneworks building and its Art Nouveau inscription.

FRIARS WALK

Railway days: the town's first railway terminal was built where the magistrates' court now stands.

A short stroll along Friars Walk takes us through several hundred years of local history. The land occupied by the magistrates' court was part of the medieval Franciscan friary which also encompassed the Fitzroy House site – we shall meet one of its relics shortly. In 1846 the London, Brighton and South Coast Railway established its first railway station here, although problems with manouevring the trains in tight spaces prompted them to build another one in 1857 close to the present station. The Friars Walk building was knocked down in 1967.

Crossing the road we come to Broomans Lane, with a squat little building on its corner which has an interesting history. In the early 1860s the turkish bath movement, evangelically promoted by David Urquhart, was all the rage throughout the country. The newly widowed Hannah Fitzroy, no thought of a library in her head at the time, had offered the town several thousand pounds for public baths, and Burwood Godlee JP was appointed chairman of a committee charged with building and running them. By chance Godlee met a close friend of Urquhart on the Brighton train, and he became convinced that Lewes needed a hot-air turkish bath rather than what he called a 'water trough'. The controversy over what kind of bath to build seems to have frightened Mrs Fitzroy off. She built the library instead, while Godlee and six other subscribers formed a new company to create the turkish bath. It opened in 1863 and enjoyed a moderate success before the company was wound up in 1882.

The turkish bath served the people of Lewes for almost 20 years.

The much persecuted Lewes Quakers were visited by their founder, George Fox, in 1655, and William Penn, the Quaker who gave his name to Pennsylvania, worshipped with them when their meeting house was in Puddle Lane, Cliffe. They moved to their present elegant headquarters, hung with red mathematical tiles, in 1784.

There are 38 humble headstones in the grounds, most of them for the Rickman family, who were well-to-do brewers and merchants. The best known of the family , for reasons other than trade, is

The Quaker meeting house has a modest, undecorated interior. Most of the gravestones (right) commemorate the Rickman family.

Thomas 'Clio' (1761–1834), also grandly known as 'the Citizen of the World'. A friend of the revolutionary writer Thomas Paine, who lodged with him in Lewes for a time, he was a poet who left the Friends after marrying a non-Quaker and is therefore *not* buried here. His verse is largely forgettable, but a lively and amusing epitaph at Newhaven to the brewer Thomas Tipper is often quoted: it ends 'Be better, wiser, laugh more if you can.'

Further along the street we come to an archway from the former friary. The Grey Friars had settled in Lewes by 1241,

relying largely on charity to sustain them in their work of preaching to the common man and woman, hearing confessions and burying the dead. They seem to have had a good reputation overall, but once the political knives were out for them at the Dissolution they had no chance: charges were concocted against them and they were accused of treason. The house was closed down in 1538.

An archway from the friary.

The Pinwell spring, which gushed at the western side of the street, was doubtless used by the friars, but the authorities kept it available for public use, too. By the 19th century it was poorly maintained – it had to be cleared of rubbish in 1812, when it was 'in a ruinous state', and again in 1839, when an iron pump was installed. In 1874 the pump was moved to the other side of the road and a drinking fountain was erected by public subscription – it still stands against the wall of All Saints church today.

The Pinwell drinking fountain.

All Saints church is now an arts and youth centre.

One of the works of art in the churchyard.

In the All Saints churchyard venerable chest tombs, urns and obelisks mingle with ingenious and colourful modern sculptures. The church, now redundant, shows obvious evidence of having been added to over the years. The west tower, made of flint, dates from the 16th century, but the Brighton-based architect Amon Wilds created a long brick nave in 1806, while in 1883 more flint was introduced when a new east end, with transepts, was built. The idea was to replace Wilds' work, but the money ran out before the job could be finished.

Inside there are galleries supported by thin iron columns. On the walls you can see two Jacobean 'kneelers' – memorials featuring kneeling man-and-wife effigies. The one in the tower is to Robert Hassard, who had the wonderful title Keeper of the King's Jewel House. The other, in the nave, is to John Stansfield, a wealthy exporter of iron and grain and importer of salt, fish and wine. He was the grandfather of the

The monument to John Stansfield and his wife, Jane.

diarist John Evelyn, who spent several boyhood years with his grandparents at the Grange in Lewes. Stansfield was the major financial backer of the church at South Malling, and the young Evelyn laid one of its foundation stones in 1626.

All Saints now functions as an arts and youth centre, and – since the town lacks one – as a cinema, too.

SCHOOL HILL

Although School Hill (the lower part of the High Street) runs up from Eastgate corner only as far as the war memorial, this section of our walk continues the short distance to the Station Street crossroads. The name, it seems, has nothing to do with education.

The former creamery is now the local Liberal Democrats HQ.

A historian writing in 1795 claimed that the Saxons named it for its coolness, the initial 'S' having been added later – a suggestion that would 'not appear improbable to those who have experienced the constant draught of air that prevails along this street at every season.'

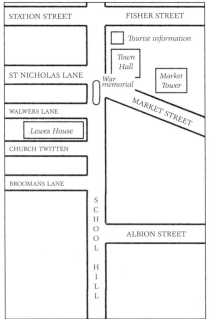

There have been some modern disasters in this street – the *Sussex Express* on your left and the estate agents' building on the corner of the attractively terraced Albion Street – but at least the pretty facade of School Hill Creamery has been listed and saved: Albert Reed was the dairyman here from 1922.

There are Georgian fronts aplenty both here and further up the High Street, but many of them conceal much older Tudor buildings, and several have medieval undercrofts. School Hill saw some major developments at the turn of the 18th and 19th centuries, and Lewes House (headquarters of the district council) followed the trend: although it can be traced back to 1609, it had a new front added after 1812. The building's main claim to fame, however, is that it was the home of the American art connoisseur Edward Perry Warren  between 1890 and 1928, and so became the focus of the great, and ridiculous, scandal over Rodin's sculpture The Kiss.

Warren, a millionaire with a passion for antiquities, acquired the lease in 1890, after searching for a house that was spacious enough for both his art collection and his beloved dogs and horses, and he was to buy the property outright in 1913. He furnished Lewes House with the finest antique furniture, hung the walls with tapestries and primitive paintings and displayed priceless bronzes, ivories and vases in every room. He commissioned Rodin, a friend and frequent visitor, to make The Kiss, based on

The back of Lewes House, from the garden.

a work he had already completed. It was finished in 1906, brought to Lewes and installed in Warren's coach house, Thebes. Eight years later he offered it to the town for display, and it was given a prominent place in the town hall's assembly room.

The first indignity inflicted upon the statue was its use as a vantage point for troops, billeted in the town hall, to get a better view of boxing matches held there. Then, in 1917, the appropriately named Miss Fowler–Tutt persuaded the council that the amorousness of the two lovers would be too much for injured soldiers, newly returned from the battlefront, to bear. (She also had realistic nipples removed from the war memorial's angel.) The Kiss was returned to Thebes, where it languished until Warren's death in 1928. Today it can be seen in the Tate Gallery. Its return to Lewes town hall for a special exhibition in 1999 served as a reminder of what we might have enjoyed for all time had the council only managed to play its cards right.

Thebes, the former coach house where Rodin's Kiss was kept, now stages art exhibitions.

Lewes House sits between two of the many ancient twittens which are among the most attractive features of the town – narrow lanes between high flint walls running down from the High Street to the south. (They had their counterparts on the other side until the Normans developed the castle and its environs.) Thebes is in Walwer's Lane, but Church Twitten on the other side of the house is a particularly fine example – and well worth a detour.

A view along Church Twitten.

We've mentioned mathematical tiles before, and opposite Lewes House you can see a particularly fine example of their use. Nos 199 and 200 date from 1790, just the time when it was fashionable to hang them on bow windows such as these. They were hung on timber frames to simulate brick, which was regarded as vastly superior to the old timber-framing of an earlier era. They aren't difficult to spot once you get your eye in (M-tiles are, of course, much thinner than bricks), although even the great Nikolaus Pevsner nodded here, in his Buildings of England *Sussex* volume, describing this handsome pair as 'red brick'.

Mathematical tiles at 199–200 School Hill.

The war memorial, erected in 1922, is the focal point for the famous Lewes bonfire celebrations each November 5.

The war memorial at the top of School Hill.

Here the five bonfire societies, dressed in a dazzling array of costumes, march with their banners, their crosses and their accompanying musical bands as the evening's drama unfolds. For each, a bugler plays the Last Post as wreaths are laid to remember the fallen.

To understand the underlying passion of the occasion you need only walk across to the town hall, where a plaque records the death of 17 Protestants during the reign of Bloody Queen Mary – ten of them burned at the stake at a spot just a few yards away. (Up on the hill above Cliffe is a memorial raised to them in 1901.) The anti-Catholic nature of the occasion was established after the Gunpowder Plot, when the strong Puritan element in Lewes paraded with effigies of Guy Fawkes and the Pope and his cardinals. It wasn't an unbroken tradition, but in the 1840s, with anti-Catholic feeling once again to the fore, the bonfire boys revived the 'No Popery' venom. Today the societies take care to emphasise that the Pope triumphantly blown to pieces at the end of their extravagant firework displays is an historic figure rather

than the present incumbent.

IN THE VAULTS BENEATH THIS BUILDING WERE IMPRISONED TEN OF THE SEVENTEEN PROTESTANT MARTYRS WHO WERE BURNED AT THE STAKE WITHIN A FEW YARDS OF THIS SITE 1555-1557 THEIR NAMES ARE RECORDED ON THE MEMORIAL TO BE SEEN ON CLIFFE HILL

"FAITHFUL UNTO DEATH"

Back in the 1550s the Star Inn stood on this site, and a flight of ancient steps takes you (by invitation only) to the 14th century undercroft in which those brave souls are said to have been held before being led out to their terrible death.

A more visible staircase is the fine Elizabethan example that leads up from the ground floor inside the main entrance of the town hall. This was originally at Slaugham Place, some 15 miles to the north-west, but Thomas Sergison brought it here in the 1730s when he was rebuilding the inn as a base for his Tory followers. (His Whig rivals were led by Thomas Pelham, Duke of Newcastle, who owned – among much else – the Pelham Arms.)

The town hall, the plaque to the martyrs and the elegantly carved Elizabethan staircase.

The town hall in its present form dates from 1893, when Samuel Denman created the distinctive red facade with its five attractive keystones, including Ceres, the goddess of agriculture, and Bacchus, the god of wine.

The tourist information office next door is housed in what was at one time the Star coffee house, but which in the 1850s became the double-fronted shop of the shoe manufacturer Albion Russell. His daughter Elizabeth married George Bromley from Hastings, and the couple developed the famous shoe chain.

Bacchus – a keystone on the Town Hall facade.

MARKET STREET

The Market Tower of 1792.

As you turn down Market Street from the war memorial you'll see the tower of the former provision market with the borough coat of arms in terracotta on the front. This is thought to be the work of the Heathfield stonemason Jonathan Harmer, whose distinctive work (cherubs, vases, baskets of fruit) adorns gravestones throughout the east of Sussex: there's a display of his work in the Anne of Cleves museum.

Inside the tower is the bell Gabriel, cast in 1555 and until 1761 hanging in the belfry of St Nicholas church, which stood where the war memorial is today. The bell is still rung on special occasions.

Julian Bell's portrait of Thomas Paine in the Market Tower.

On a wall beneath the tower is a fine modern painting of Thomas Paine by the Lewes-based artist Julian Bell. It depicts the great 'apostle of freedom' pointing west to America while the River Seine wends its way towards a burning Bastille in Paris: Paine inspired both the American and French revolutions.

We shall discover further Paine associations later on our journey, but this is a good point at which to consider his links with the town. Born in Norfolk in 1737, he became a riding officer in the Lewes area for the unpopular Board of Excise. He lodged with the tobacconist Samuel Ollive in the High Street and, after his death, ran the business with Ollive's daughter Elizabeth – they later married. Paine was a keen member of the Lewes Bowling Green Club and a fiery political debater at the Headstrong Club, based at the White Hart, where he argued for women's rights and the abolition of slavery.

It was also while in Lewes that Paine wrote his first pamphlet, arguing for a salary increase for excise officers. He soon moved to London in an attempt to further this cause and there he met the American inventor, scientist and printer Benjamin Franklin, who gave him a letter of introduction to his son-in-law in Philadelphia. The shop in Lewes was closed, and Paine began his new career as journalist, polemicist and author, his books including *Rights of Man* and *Common Sense*. Much vilified though they were at the time, many of his ideas are common currency today. We like to think that Lewes played its part.

FISHER STREET

Lewes once had seven breweries, not to speak of something like ten times that number of pubs, and there's a record of Obadiah Elliott brewing in Fisher Street as early as 1739. Thomas Beard took over the business in 1811, and his company operated here until 1958, when the plant closed – Harvey's brewed for the firm on a contract business until 1986. Several substantial buildings in Lewes were threatened during the 1960s and 70s (some of them by a proposed 'relief road' which would have shouldered its way

through the centre of the town on stilts) and the Star Brewery was saved only by dogged campaigning from the Friends of Lewes and other conservationists. Today it's a thriving arts and crafts centre, with painters, potters and book-binders in residence. Do go in and look around.

Approaching from the High Street you pass the council offices of 1913 with pretty plaster friezes along the facade – Sussex oxen pulling a

The former Star Brewery owned by Beard & Co now houses workshops and studios.

Plaster frieze of Sussex oxen on the council offices.

plough and a harvest waggon. Next comes the Lamb (one of several Lewes inn signs painted by Julian Bell) and then a little row of shops, restaurants and hairdressers with, among them, a working forge. An old sign still hangs above the door, its wording reminding us of a local attraction that was first recorded in 1751 but which disappeared well within living memory. There was a thriving racecourse on the downs west of the town in the Georgian era (the first recorded meeting was in 1751), when 'the fashion' – including the Prince Regent – would visit from neighbouring Brighton. Everything turned sour in the 1960s when the Jockey Club decided to reduce the number of courses in the country. A notice was posted at the last meeting on September 14, 1964: 'A small racecourse is an essential part of the English racing scene . . . The racecourse is being closed against the wishes of the management and of many people who believe that the decision will be regretted in the future.'

The old Star Forge sign in Fisher Street declares 'Race horses & hunters a speciality.' Racing has gone, but the forge is still busy.

HIGH STREET

Goring coat of arms in Pelham House.

Our next section of the High Street takes us from the Station Street crossroads to the castle. On both sides there are fine old buildings, large and small, with a variety of facing materials, and once again narrow twittens run down to the south.

A short distance along the first of them, St Andrews Lane, is Pelham House. This was built in 1579 as a town mansion for George Goring of Danny in Hurstpierpoint, and his coat of arms can be seen on the celebrated carved panelling in one of the rooms. Until recently the house was owned by East Sussex county council and used for meetings and functions, but it's now in private hands as a restaurant, conference centre and hotel.

The White Hart hotel by the crossroads was bought by the powerful Pelham family in 1568, but it was a hostelry by the 1720s. In 1759 the landlord, William Verall, having trained under the Duke of Newcastle's French chef, published his book *A Complete System*

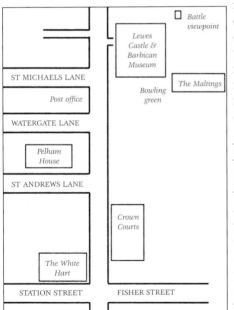

THOMAS PAINE 1737-1809
HERE EXPOUNDED HIS
REVOLUTIONARY POLITICS.
THIS INN IS REGARDED AS
A CRADLE OF AMERICAN
INDEPENDENCE WHICH HE
HELPED TO FOUND WITH
PEN AND SWORD.

Clio Rickman wrote that 'the White Hart evening club was the resort of a social and intelligent circle who, out of fun, seeing that disputes often ran very warm and high, frequently had what they called the "Headstrong Book". This was no other than an old Greek Homer which was sent the morning after a debate vehemently maintained to the most obstinate haranguer in the club.'

of Cookery. The Sheriff's Room on the first floor was the setting for elaborate banquets held by the high constables and other officials. It was also the headquarters of the Headstrong Club where, as we have seen, Thomas Paine debated politics. In the heyday of coach services between Lewes and London this was the leading inn in town, with stabling for as many as a hundred horses. Tudor fireplaces and oak panelling still give the place a special flavour.

On the opposite side of the road are the Crown Courts, originally built in 1812 as the county hall. The Coade stone figures in the panels above, depict Wisdom, Justice and Mercy. The worst crimes in Sussex are tried here, and a familiar sight is the throng of journalists outside amid a cluster of cameras and microphones when a verdict is expected.

Next door is Newcastle House – although it's not Thomas Pelham's imposing 18th century building of that name, which was dismantled in 1928. A panelled room and the original staircase survive, as does the 'Seize the Day' sundial of 1717 high on the Portland stone front.

Above: The Crown Courts.

Right: Carpe Diem sundial on the pediment of Newcastle House.

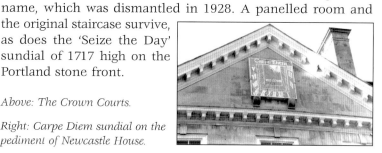

THE CASTLE

William the Conqueror divided the south of England among his friends and trusty lieutenants, and the Lewes area was given to William de Warenne. He built his castle on the site of the Saxon 'burh' that had been raised by Alfred the Great as part of his defences against the Danes. It's unusual in having two separate mounds, or mottes – he probably established his initial wooden structure on Brack Mount to the east, soon afterwards building the much more solid keep of flint and stone on the other one. (Both of them, each with a core of chalk blocks, already existed and are among a pattern of early mounds in Lewes which are as yet unexplained.) As a model in one of the castle rooms helpfully demonstrates, there would have been a walled courtyard, or bailey, between the two mottes. The towers were added in the 13th century and the formidable barbican entrance tower about a hundred years later.

The castle is owned by the Sussex Archaeological Society, which will sell you a combined ticket which also gives you entrance to the Barbican House museum (it has a town model with sound-and-light performances throughout the day) and the Anne of Cleves House museum in Southover (*page 56*).

A model of the castle, showing its unusual feature – the two mottes. The shell keep with its towers stands on the one on the right

Many medieval castles never knew a genuine battle, but this one faced an assault by the great crusader knight Simon de Montfort on May 14th 1264. King Henry III and his army, involved in skirmishes with de Montfort and his rebellious barons for several weeks, had marched into the town a few

The mighty barbican offers the first view of the castle from the High Street.

days before. It was owned by the 7th Earl de Warenne, a former friend of de Montfort who now sided with the king.

The rebel army of some 10,000 men, having camped around Fletching and Piltdown, came over the Downs under cover of darkness and gathered on Offham Hill at first light. What followed was bloody in the extreme. The royalist cavalry under Prince Edward swept out of the town and put the left flank of de Montfort's army to the sword, some of the hapless, fleeing victims being slaughtered four miles from the town. Edward's reckless pursuit of them was, however, to prove his own side's

A plaque showing the battle formations, with Offham Hill beyond.

downfall. It left the royalists depleted, and de Montfort's troops

The shell keep of Lewes Castle.

charged down the slopes and fought their way into the town, much of which was devastated in the fighting. The king's brother, Prince Richard, was captured hiding in a windmill, while Henry himself found sanctuary in the priory.

These were callous times. Up on Malling Down, overlooking the town to the east, nine skeletons were recently unearthed – 'well-built males,' an archaeologist reported, 'who had their hands tied behind their backs and appear to have been decapitated and then flung into a shallow mass grave.

There is also evidence from skull fragments above ground that some of the skulls may have been displayed on spikes above the grave.' Almost certainly these were prisoners taken during the battle and executed without pity.

The upshot of the barons' victory was that the king was forced to sign the Mise of Lewes, a document with echoes of the earlier Magna Carta, giving the chartered boroughs representation in parliament. This milestone on the long road to democracy made de Montfort the most powerful man in the kingdom, but he was unable to enjoy his triumph for long – he was killed at the Battle of Evesham the following year.

Walking under the Barbican you come to the ancient bowling green on your right – it was formerly the castle tilting ground – and then The Maltings. This long, low building was built for Castle Brewery in 1852 and now houses the county record office.

Up on the left, with a view across to Offham Hill, is a plaque which explains how the Battle of Lewes was fought.

The bowling green from the castle, with Brack Mount visible behind The Maltings.

THE PELLS

We take a diversion from the High Street to visit the Pells area, north of the castle down by the river. From The Maltings follow the steep slope down Castle Banks and cross the road by the Elephant and Castle public house into Abinger Place. You pass plaques on your left marking the places by the former Saxon town wall where the gallows and the manor pound once lay.

Straight ahead of you is the church of St John-sub-Castro ('under the castle'), on a raised site inside the north-west corner of the wall. There were once several large mounds in this area, and archaeologists and antiquarians still debate their possible pre-Christian significance. It's also thought that the Romans had a camp here, and there's a plaque to make the claim on the terrace called the Fosse along Lancaster Street.

The church dates from 1839, when it became the first major Neo-Gothic building in Lewes. It replaced a smaller and more attractive Saxon church, one of its doorways still to be seen incorporated in the chancel wall. A more remarkable relic is set into an outside wall of the aisle – the original chancel arch with its

Pells Pool

Pells Lake

PELHAM TERRACE

BROOK STREET

St John-sub-Castro church

The Fosse

TORONTO TERRACE

LANCASTER STREET

ST JOHNS TERRACE

ABINGER PLACE

Site of gallows

Elephant & Castle

medieval Lombardic lettering. What it tells us is that a Danish warrior, Prince Magnus, became an anchorite here – voluntarily locked up in a cell and throwing himself upon the charity of local people for his food and wellbeing.

Above left: the curious arch commemorating Prince Magnus, a Danish anchorite.. The drawing of it in Camden's Britannia *in 1586 inspired generations of architectural draughtsmen.*

Left: St John-sub-Castro church replaced a Saxon building which had become too small for the rapidly growing population of Lewes' 'New Town'.

In the church porch is a memorial to Sax Rohmer, the creator of the fictional Dr Fu Manchu, but anyone who enjoys gravestones and memorials will make first for the churchyard. The headstone to Mark Sharp is justly celebrated, although time has worn its stone to such an extent that it is hard to find and its carving is much less distinct than it was when the drawing on the right was made. Sharp, who died in 1747, was a carpenter,

A carpenter's gravestone.

and the mason decorated the stone with the tools of his trade – plane, hammer, saw and so on.

The memorial to Finnish prisoners of the Crimean War is, by contrast, impossible to miss. This large obelisk was funded by

Czar Alexander II, who was Grand Duke of Finland, in 1877. Hundreds of captured soldiers (Russians and Swedes as well as Finns) were held in the former House of Correction in North Street, and 28 died here. There were escapes (one man was picked up in the nearby King's Arm's, where he was drinking a glass of rum), but they generally got on well with their captors. When the last 326 prisoners left in 1856, they were marched off by the Lewes Saxon Horn Band, and the locals gathered to wish them well. Some of the wooden toys they made and sold while incarcerated in Lewes can be seen in the Anne of Cleves museum.

The obelisk to Finnish prisoners of war, raised by Czar Aexander II.

Below the church the land falls away to marshy ground that fringes the Ouse. The L-shaped lake with its small islands and resident ducks lies on a plot of land given to the town by John Rowe more than 400 years ago. At one time there was a paper mill on the site, but old photographs show its use for regattas and other events in the Victorian era, when it was described as 'a beautiful piece of ornamental water, fringed with trees.'

Next to it is the al fresco Pells Pool, which claims to be the oldest of its kind in the country. Fed by a natural spring, its water can feel rather cold, but campaigners have helped it survive competition from the modern leisure centre.

The land on which the Pells lake lies was first given to the people of Lewes in 1603. The open-air pool was built in 1860.

41

HIGH STREET

We rejoin the High Street immediately west of the castle, standing outside the house where Dr Gideon Mantell lived. Amon Wilds created it for him in 1819 by merging the central two units of what had been a terrace of four houses: the ammonite capitals on the pilasters of the porch were the architect's punning motif, and they can be seen in the many parts of Brighton which he developed.

Mantell, a medical man, is best known for discovering, and naming, the fossil bones of the iguanodon in Tilgate Forest. (A later amateur geologist, Charles Dawson who lived in Castle Lodge just beyond the Barbican gate, was to be at the centre of the Piltdown Man scandal.) A driven man, Mantell was both a geologist and an antiquarian. In 1814 he was digging in his garden in order to shore up the castle walls and prevent them falling into it when he found a Roman urn with the bones of a cockerel, a boar and a

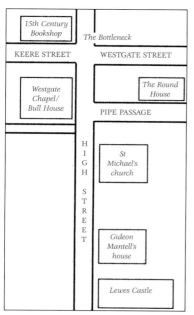

Dr Gideon Mantell's house at Castle Place.

42

horse, together with oyster and mussel shells. He was unable to excavate further for fear that the castle tower would topple. Inside the house Mantell kept his renowned geological collections, later sold to the British Museum.

On the other side of the street there's a plaque to a doctor whose fame rests on his professional expertise rather than on his extra-curricular activities. Richard Russell is widely credited with inspiring Brighton's development as a resort by advocating 'the

sea water cure'. He first practised in the High Street here, before moving to the coast where most of his patients were.

St Michael's, further up the High Street, has a Georgian facade, but its round flint tower (one of only three in Sussex) dates from around the 12th century.

St Michael's church has the figure of the archangel on its round flint tower.

Inside, don't miss the fine Renaissance monument of 1559 to Sir Nicholas Pelham, an ancestor of the Duke of Newcastle. Some 14 years before his death he had fought off an invasion by French marauders near Seaford, and the event is remembered in typically punning Tudor fashion in his epitaph:

> *What time ye French sought to have sackt Seafoord*
> *This Pelham did repell them back aboord.*

The small churchyard is worth a visit, too, with its chest tombs among the trees. Just outside the north door is a stone which commemorates 15-year-old Thomas Hodson Plummer, who died in 1813: its verse quatrain ends with the desperate conviction that 'Twas Heavens high will; its will be done'.

The most unusual stone is one with concentric writing to the family of Robert Buckland. It's dated 1631, which appears to

make it the earliest churchyard memorial in the county, but the style suggests that it may have been erected later.

Left: The Pelham memorial in St Michael's church includes a typical Tudor pun.

Below: The Buckland headstone carries the earliest date in any Sussex churchyard.

Across the street a little further up is Bull House, built as an inn during the 15th century. Sir Henry Goring of Ovingdean restructured it as a townhouse in 1583 (adding an overhang on curved brackets, a gabled porch and two rather strange wooden satyrs), although it reverted to its original use during the following century.

It was here that Thomas Paine lodged between 1768 and 1774 (*page 28*), taking a room on the upper floor and marrying the daughter of the owner – tobacconist Samuel Ollive.

Bull House, as the plaque and lettering proclaim, was the home of Thomas Paine. This 15th century building was originally the Bull Inn. Its two carved satyrs were added by Sir Henry Goring in 1583.

The sign outside Westgate Chapel announces that it's a 'meeting place for groups working for justice, peace and responsible stewardship of the Earth.'

Local Presbyterians converted the rear of Bull House into the Westgate Chapel in 1700 (it was known as the Bull Meeting), and it remains a home of the 'low church' Unitarians and Methodists to this day. During the Second World War the chapel was dealt a blow with the death of John Every of the Phoenix Iron Works, who had long supported it, and members had to share a minister with Ditchling and,  later, Brighton. In 1987, however, the One World Centre opened in the chapel, giving it a welcome financial security.

We now approach the dog-leg which is known to locals as the Bottleneck, and on the far side of Keere Street is the 15th Century Bookshop with, set into its facade, a milestone whose

The half-timbered facade of the 15th century bookshop, with an old milestone set into it.

wording reveals its venerability: 'Brighthelmstone' was an early spelling of Brighton which passed out of common currency in the early 19th century.

During the 18th century the Harman and Neeves families ran a business making tobacco pipes in these premises.

PIPE PASSAGE

The pipe-making industry, using imported clay, gave its name to the twitten which runs north of the High Street a little to the east of the Bottleneck. During the 1820s Henry Pink and William Privet had a kiln just off Pipe Passage, and its traces are visible below the steps. Once you've climbed those steps you're on the old sentry walk along the town's defensive wall.

At the end of Pipe Passage lies The Round House, which sits on the base of a town mill built by public subscription in 1802 when the price of bread was exceptionally

The Round House was briefly owned by Virginia Woolf.

high and many families were in desperate straits: the idea was 'to grind corn at a moderate price for ready money'. The smock mill lasted on the site only until 1819, when a team of bullocks hauled it up the hill to a spot near the crossroads west of the town where the winds were more vigorous – though it had to be raised some 20ft when the prison was built next door to it. (It was taken down in the 1920s and the base was adapted as a tack store for the local stables.)

The brick foundations in Pipe Passage were used as the base for the attractive little house that stands there today. In 1919 the writer Virginia Woolf was so taken with The Round House that she bought it on a whim. ('It's the butt end of an old windmill,' she wrote to Dora Carrington, 'so that all the rooms are completely round or semi-circular.') Once she had calmed down she realised that a home in the country suited her purposes much better, so she sold it and bought Monks House at Rodmell instead.

WESTGATE STREET

Turn into Westgate Street for a glimpse of the original town walls, rebuilt on their Saxon foundations after the Battle of Lewes. The area now given over to a car park was once covered with a cluster of humble cottages that were pulled down as part of a slum clearance scheme in the 1930s.

The White Lion inn also stood here. The Friends of Lewes Society later rescued the pub sign and had it erected on the wall – it's thought to have been made by Abraham Larwill, tinplate worker, brazier and wire worker to the Prince of Wales, no less.

The White Lion inn sign.

KEERE STREET

We turn down Keere Street to make another diversion from the High Street. Note the water-rolled flints forming the watercourse at the centre of this celebrated twitten: known as 'petrified kidneys', they were probably barged up the Ouse from the beach at Newhaven. Among the attractive cottages note St Michael's Court, formerly almshouses.

Down this steep slope (as a sign on the street lamp at the bottom records) the Prince Regent, later King George IV, is said to have ridden a coach-and-four for a wager – perilous, certainly, but just the kind of thing to tempt a Regency buck. 'Prinnie' visited Lewes often, to attend the races and to see his friend Col William Newton at the Grange.

The Prince Regent is said to have ridden down the steep incline of Keere Street in a coach-and-four in order to win a bet.

SOUTHOVER

The Southover area of the town, down below the High Street and fringed by low-lying fields which regularly flooded before the river was canalised late in the 18th century, was once a separate entity – like Cliffe, it was incorporated into the borough of Lewes as recently as 1881. The old Saxon wall came down Keere Street from the west gate and turned above what is now Southover Road, and a large section of it can be seen (*page 52*) as you stand by Southover Grange, looking up.

Old buildings have often been used as quarries, and William Newton (steward to the Earl of Dorset) had a supply of fine Caen stone readily to hand when he built the Grange in 1572. A short way off lay the dismantled priory founded by William de Warenne and his wife Gundrada after the Conquest, and this was irresistible. Newton's original staircase can still be seen inside –

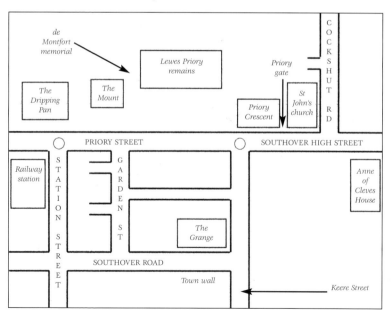

A section of the old town wall rears up on the corner of Keere Street and Southover Road, opposite the Grange.

the building now serves, among other things, as the local register office. One of the chimneypieces has the date 1572 on it, while another two from the early 16th century may have come from the prior's lodging at the priory. The beautifully kept grounds also contain stones from the priory, although it's by no means certain that the rather comical monk's head above one of the arches came from the site – some experts have suggested a later date for it.

Monk's head in Southover Grange Gardens.

The diarist John Evelyn lived here as a boy with his maternal grandfather John Stansfield (*page 21*). At the age of nine he enrolled at the Free Grammar School in Southover and he was educated there until he went to university.

Southover Grange, built in 1572 and now owned by Lewes District Council. The gardens, with their ornamental trees, shrub borders and colourful beds, are a favourite retreat for Lewesians.

Another relic of the priory can be seen at the western end of Priory Crescent a little to the south – the remains of the gatehouse.

The Crescent, which dates from the 1830s, has 20 bays in stucco and yellow brick. It's unusual for Lewes, and architectural authorities have been rather sniffy about it, describing it as 'Lewes' stab at grandeur' and 'townish and out of place'. It was built on the monks' former cemetery, and a guide of 1846 reported that 'it was singular to observe the workmen, when strangers approached them, taking out of their pockets a handful of

A gateway from the former priory survives alongside Priory Crescent.

Priory Crescent was built on the site of the monks' cemetery.

teeth, which were as perfect as when first buried, which they offered for sale, and sculls [*sic*] when they could get them out without their pick or bar having broken them, and readily disposing of them from 6d to 2s; the jaw bones with a good set of teeth they expected 6d for.' The teeth would find their way into new sets of dentures.

Fish weathervane on St John the Baptist.

St John the Baptist church was formerly the hospital at the north gate of the priory. In the south chapel you'll find memorials to William and Gundrada de Warenne which have a curious history. The priory was knocked down without ceremony during the Dissolution of the Monasteries, and the two lead cists containing the bones of the founders lay forgotten until the day in October 1845 that navvies were working on the site for the new railway. Fortunately the boxes had the Christian names on their lids or they might have been lost for ever. (Today it takes some believing that a cutting 40ft wide through the historic monument should have been allowed in the first place.)

The treasure of them all, however, is the black slab of Tournai marble to Gundrada, carved around 1145. This disappeared at the Dissolution, only to be discovered in 1775 upside down in Isfield church where worshippers had, unknowing, been walking over it for some two hundred years. Will William's slab ever be found?

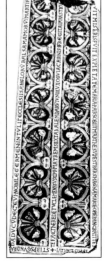

The beautiful black marble slab to Gundrada, lost for hundreds of years, was found in an East Sussex church where it was being used as a paving slab.

Before visiting the ruins we'll first walk along Southover High Street. It's lined with attractive old buildings, but Anne of Cleves House stands out. The front porch carries the date 1599 and the initials of the then owner, John Saxpes, but it was already getting on for a hundred years old when he added the three-storied west wing and this porch. There's heavy Horsham slate on the roof, and the frontage includes brick, flint, hung tile and stone.

Anne of Cleves, alas, never lived here: as owner of the manor of Southover she received an annual rent for the freehold. The house is now owned by the Sussex Archaeological Society, and a combined ticket gives access to its interesting local history collection (including an informative display about the Wealden iron industry), the castle and the Barbican House museum.

The priory ruins are found off Cockshut Road, and they're a sorry sight – particularly if you're aware that the magnificent priory church was, with a length of almost 450ft, larger even than Chichester Cathedral. The de Warennes had visited the great

Anne of Cleves House is a typical Wealden timber-framed building of the early 16th century. It houses an excellent museum of local history.

The Priory of St Pancras: its church was larger than Chichester Cathedral.

abbey of Cluny in Burgundy around 1075 and immediately offered to build the order a foundation at Southover. The work was clearly carried out speedily, because Gundrada was buried here as early as 1085, having died in childbirth, and William three years later.

As we have seen, the great priory was first dismantled in the Dissolution and later dissected by the railway line. Today its ruins can be viewed only through a wire fence (turn left just before the South Down Tennis Club), although a recent Lottery grant offers hope of better things to come. Some stones from the original church (later the infirmary church) can be seen, but the foundations of the second, much more substantial and lavishly decorated church lie under a former market garden to the north. Also visible are the stumps of various domestic buildings, their flint and chalk cores exposed because most of the Caen stone covering has fallen away or been taken from the site – the dorter, or dormitory, with a series of undercrofts (previously vaulted), the rere-dorters, or lavatories, and part of the refectory wall.

A short distance from the ruins is the de Montfort memorial which the local MP, Sir Tufton Beamish, presented to the town to mark the 700th anniversary of the Battle of Lewes in 1964. Designed by Enzo Plazzotta as a giant helmet, it has scenes from the battle encircling the bronze chaplet at the top.

de Montfort memorial.

And then a mystery. Continue into the Convent Field and you'll see a large grass-covered mound beyond the bowling green. This is the Mount. We know that it was here by the 15th century, but what was its purpose? There have been many theories – was it another castle motte, perhaps; the base of a windmill; a platform raised by the monks for outdoor services; or a 'harvest hill' climbed by neolithic people to commune with their fertility gods? A more prosaic possibility is that it was simply the spoil-heap of the neighbouring Dripping Pan, now the home of Lewes Football Club.

But here's another mystery: why was the Pan dug out? One suggestion is that it was a medieval salt-pan, taking water from the estuarine marshes and producing salt through evaporation.

The Mount: a spoil-heap or a hill created for religious observance?

ST ANNE'S HILL

We return to the Bottleneck now, and walk west up the incline of St Anne's Hill for the last stage of our journey. Immediately on our right is the Old Grammar School, with its frontage of knapped flints (*page 60*). The former Free Grammar School moved to this site in 1714 – it had been the lodgings for the headmaster, and it's thought that the steep and arduous climb up Keere Street every day persuaded him to move the whole school here – and the building was remodelled in a neo-Tudor style in 1851. Numbers were never large, with 51 boys on the roll in 1861 and only 23 four years later. When the original school closed in 1885, its endowments were converted into exhibitions for children living within five miles of the town. Continuity was achieved when a former mayor, Thomas Reader White, took over, and today it's an independent co-educational school with a growing reputation.

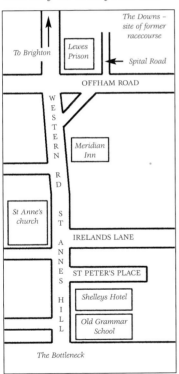

A little further up the street is Shelleys Hotel (*page 60*). Back in 1527 this was the Vine Inn, but some 50 years later the Southover brewer Thomas Pelland rebuilt the front of it, adding the Renaissance porch which carries both his initials and the date. (You can see his inn sign – a nude Bacchus on a barrel with swags of grapes – at the Anne of Cleves museum.) In 1588 Lord Buckhurst, a cousin of Queen Elizabeth, bought the inn, but in

Two fine porches along St Anne's Hill.

Right: Shelleys Hotel, formerly the Vine Inn, has a porch of 1577. The wealthy Shelley family (the poet was related, but never came here) created an elegant town house from the late 17th century.

Below: The Lewes Old Grammar School building was given a make-over in 1851. The Free Grammar School moved to the site from Southover in 1714, and it has been an educational establishment ever since.

1663 it went to the opposition, as it were: Henry Shelley – an ardent Whig supporter whom Charles II had sacked as a JP – bought the place and converted it into his town house. One of his descendants remodelled the facade in 1763, when the house was the height of fashion, with a pillared entrance hall and a domed stairwell. The Prince Regent visited, as did Dr Samuel Johnson, who allegedly rid himself of a child's chatter by hoisting her into the branches of a cherry tree and leaving her there. The building

reverted to a hotel in 1932, since when it has catered for contemporary Prinnie equivalents such as Marilyn Monroe and Arthur Miller.

The punning Nevill armorial bearings in St Peter's Place: 'Ne Vile Velis'.

Look into St Peter's Place as you go by. On the wall are the armorial emblems of Lord Nevill, heir to the Earl of Abergavenny. Whereas the Shelleys down the road were Whigs, Nevill was a confirmed Tory, and he was confident that the tenants of his new terrace, built in

1868, would follow suit. Unluckily for him the introduction of the secret ballot in 1872 confounded his hopes. The Latin motto, which is translated as 'Wish no evil', puns on the family name: 'Ne Vile Velis'.

We shall return to the punning theme inside St Anne's church, but there are memorials to see outside first. A few steps inside the churchyard gate on your left is

The view up St Anne's Hill to the church.

61

Benjamin the Ruler's headstone.

a small stone with an unusual inscription: 'Here Lieth the Body of litle Benjamin the Ruler died Aug 21, 1747, Aged 89.' This is another mystery. There was a churchwarden in the parish named Benjamin Ellis in 1719, but why 'the ruler'? Perhaps the 'litle' gives the clue – he may have been an amateur jockey, or 'courser' in the heyday of racing up on the Downs above the town. The records do show a Benjamin Ellis leasing Spital Farm near the racecourse.

Medhurst family 'leaping boards' in the churchyard.

We know much more about Samuel Medhurst, a millwright who in the 1820s went into business with his brother William at premises near the Black Horse in Western Road. (It was they who removed the windmill from Pipe Passage: *page 48*.) He worked on both watermills and windmills and won a high reputation for his innovative construction work – the Sussex tailpole fan-tackle (for swinging a mill into the wind) is attributed to the Medhursts.

Although he lived to 88, most of his family died young – he outlived ten of his eleven children. He worked closely with John Every of the Phoenix Iron Works, and it was he who, on Samuel's death in 1887, provided the unusual memorials to the family in the St Anne's churchyard. Fashioned in the old 'leaping board' style, they are, fittingly, made of iron.

The 12th century south arcade is the most praised part of St Anne's interior, but do look out for the punning brass in the chancel to Dr Thomas Twine, who died in 1613. The engraver couldn't resist including two snakes – entwined. 'Now that the physician is no longer here,' the distinctly over-the-top Latin inscription tells us, 'disease is all powerful on every side and rejoices in the absence of its avenger . . . Bereft of her physician Sussex languishes; and in this nearly fatal year in which he passed away, she perishes.'

The grandiloquent memorial to Dr Thomas Twine, without whom Sussex was, apparently, doomed.

We found evidence at St John-sub-Castro church (*page 39*) of an anchorite sealed up in the walls, and there's an example here, too. St Richard of Chichester left money in his will to 'the female recluse of the Blessed Mary of Westoute at Lewes', and you can peer through the bars from the chancel to see where she spent her chaste and uncomfortable life. There's also a hatch in the south chapel through which she would have received her food. Her bones were dug up during restoration work in 1927, as Mrs Henry Dudeney recorded in her diary: 'After tea Mrs Miller and I with Miss Falconer to the reburial of the bones of the anchoress at St

The anchoress' cell at St Anne's church.

Anne's. Simple affair: just a bishop in cope and mitre, a few prayers, then "May she rest in peace" and "May perpetual light shone upon her." Moved me profoundly.'

WESTERN ROAD

Lewes lies on the Greenwich Meridian, and a recent owner of the Pewter Pot along Western Road decided to capitalise on the fact and change its name to the Meridian. He also took issue with the position of a plaque earlier affixed to a nearby wall by the mayor, because he claimed to have sound evidence that the line ran through the public house itself rather than a few inconvenient feet away from it.

Left: An official Meridian plaque, placed by the mayor in July 1975.

Right: Simple but attractive marker in the pub yard.

In 1673 John Brinkhurst, a poisoner who killed himself before he could be hanged, was buried at the crossroads at the top of town 'north–south, with a stake through his heart'. Nothing so ghoulish is likely to trouble us today, but we're reminded of the seamier side of life by the presence of the prison (flint, red brick, towers, machicolations) which squats on a corner. It was built from 1850 and public hangings took place here until 1868.

If this seems a somewhat sour note on which to end, take the rough track of Spital Road up beside the gaol and strike off to your right across the Downs. Before long you come to the old racecourse, where horses are still exercised, and you'll have wonderful views back across the incomparable town you have just explored. Enjoy!

Lewes Prison.

BIBLIOGRAPHY

The following books are recommended for digging deeper into the story of Lewes than this little book is able to do. A few are out of print, but all of them can be found in the new Lewes Library off Friars Walk.

Pre-Georgian Lewes, Colin Brent, Colin Brent Books
Georgian Lewes, Colin Brent, Colin Brent Books
Lewes Past, Helen Poole, Phillimore & Co
The Buildings of England: Sussex, Nairn & Pevsner, Penguin Books
Lewes Twittens, The Friends of Lewes
The Battle of Lewes 1264, Barbara Fleming, J&KH Publishing
Thomas Paine's Lewes, Judy Moore, SB Publications
The Chronicles of the Cliffe & South Malling, Brigid Chapman, The Book Guild
A Look at Lewes –the High Street from St Anne's Church to Lewes Bridge, John Houghton, Tartarus Press
Hidden Lewes: an artist's eye for detail, Marietta Van Dyck, Pomegranate Press
A Box of Toys: An Anthology of Lewes Writings, Diana Crook, Dale House Press

Old photographs:
Victorian Lewes, Colin Brent & William Rector, Phillimore & Co
Lewes in Old Photographs, Judy Middleton, Alan Sutton
Lost Lewes, Kim Clark, SB Publications
Lewes Then & Now, Volume 1, Bill Young/Bob Cairns, SB
Lewes Then & Now, Volume 2, Bill Young/David Arscott, SB

Contemporary:
Lewes 1952–2002, The Friends of Lewes, Pomegranate Press
Our Lewes, David Arscott, Sutton Publishing

INDEX

Illustrated references are shown in **bold**.

Lewes from the top of Chapel Hill, near the golf course. Stricklands warehouse, on the far side of the River Ouse, dominates the centre of the picture. The castle can be seen at the top, with St Anne's church a little further away to its left and the Sixties bulk of County Hall further left again. The Downs rise behind, with Offham Hill off to the right.

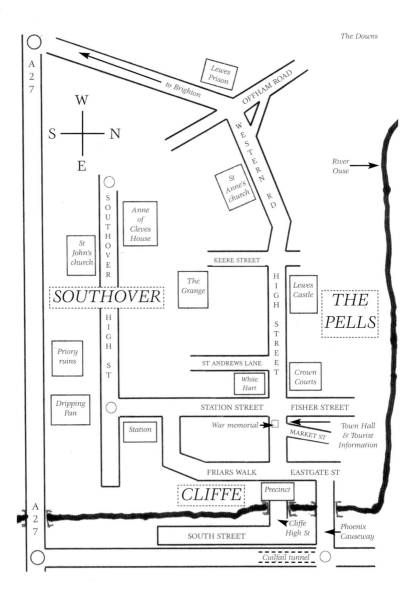

The Downs

A27

W N S E (compass)

to Brighton

Lewes Prison

OFFHAM ROAD

WESTERN RD

St Anne's church

River Ouse

SOUTHOVER HIGH ST

Anne of Cleves House

St John's church

SOUTHOVER

KEERE STREET

The Grange

HIGH STREET

Lewes Castle

THE PELLS

Priory ruins

ST ANDREWS LANE

White Hart

Crown Courts

Dripping Pan

STATION STREET

FISHER STREET

Station

War memorial

Town Hall & Tourist Information

MARKET ST

FRIARS WALK

EASTGATE ST

CLIFFE

Precinct

A27

SOUTH STREET

Cliffe High St

Phoenix Causeway

Cuilfail tunnel

72